P9-BTO-787

Recyclopedia

BOOKS BY HARRYETTE MULLEN

Sleeping with the Dictionary

Blues Baby: Early Poems

Muse & Drudge

S*PeRM**K*T

Trimmings

Tree Tall Woman

Recyclopedia

Trimmings

S*PeRM**K*T

Muse & Drudge

Harryette Mullen

Graywolf Press
SAINT PAUL, MINNESOTA

Copyright © 1991, 1992, 1995, 2006 by Harryette Mullen

Publication of this volume is made possible in part by a grant provided by
the Minnesota State Arts Board, through an appropriation by the Minnesota
State Legislature; a grant from the Wells Fargo Foundation Minnesota; and
a grant from the National Endowment for the Arts, which believes that a
great nation deserves great art. Significant support has also been provided by
the Bush Foundation; Target; the McKnight Foundation; and other generous
contributions from foundations, corporations, and individuals. To these orga-
nizations and individuals we offer our heartfelt thanks.

MINNESOTA
STATE ARTS BOARD

NATIONAL
ENDOWMENT
FOR THE ARTS

Trimmings was originally published by Tender Buttons Books, 1991.
S*PeRM**K*T was originally published by Singing Horse Press, 1992.
Muse & Drudge was originally published by Singing Horse Press, 1995.

Published by Graywolf Press
2402 University Avenue, Suite 203
Saint Paul, Minnesota 55114

All rights reserved.
www.graywolfpress.org

Published in the United States of America

ISBN-13: 978-1-55597-456-5
ISBN-10: 1-55597-456-2

2 4 6 8 9 7 5 3 1
First Graywolf Printing, 2006

Library of Congress Control Number: 2006924337

Cover design: Julie Metz
Cover art: David Hammons, *Untitled.*
Hirshhorn Museum and Sculpture Garden, Smithsonian Institution,
Joseph H. Hirshhorn Purchase Fund, 1990. Photographer: Lee Stalsworth

Contents

Preface: "Recycle This Book" / vii

Trimmings / 1

S*PeRM**K*T / 63

Muse & Drudge / 97

Recycle This Book

If the encyclopedia collects general knowledge, the recyclopedia salvages and finds imaginative uses for knowledge. That's what poetry does when it remakes and renews words, images, and ideas, transforming surplus cultural information into something unexpected. My poetry exists in part through interaction with communities of readers, writers, and scholars and also through dialogue with editors and publishers whose books and periodicals help to constitute such communities. *Recyclopedia* collects three books published originally with very small independent presses that reflect the eclectic interests of their poet founders. I am grateful to Lee Ann Brown whose Tender Buttons Books brought out *Trimmings* in 1991, and to Julia Blumenreich and the late Gil Ott whose Singing Horse Press published *S*PeRM**K*T* in 1992 and *Muse & Drudge* in 1995.

I met Lee Ann Brown when I read in the Segue poetry series at the Ear Inn in Manhattan during my first year of teaching at Cornell. Our meeting seemed inevitable: Lee Ann already knew that I was writing poems that talked back to Gertrude Stein's *Tender Buttons*; I had recently acquired one of the first Tender Buttons books Lee Ann had published, Bernadette Mayer's *Sonnets*. Lee Ann was still a graduate student at Brown University (no relation) when she started Tender Buttons Books, adopting a logo designed by Joe Brainard. She had heard of *Trimmings* from Roberto Bedoya who had invited me to read at Valencia Rose in San Francisco when I was studying at the University of California in Santa Cruz, where writers Nathaniel Mackey, Al Young, Michelle Cliff, and Lucille Clifton were teaching, and fellow student writers included Gloria Watkins (bell hooks), Alfred Arteaga, Elba Sanchez, Ken Weisner, Elizabeth Horan, Diane Rayor, and Lorna Dee Cervantes.

After graduating from the University of Texas in Austin, teaching at Austin Community College, working as a poet in the Artists in Schools program, and spending a year writing poems and stories on the Dobie ranch in Texas and at the Wurlitzer Foundation in New Mexico, I had enrolled in a graduate program in literature with the idea of teaching at a university while continuing to write poetry. Going to school in northern California introduced me to the diverse poetry communities of the Bay Area. Later I became acquainted with many writers and artists on the east coast when I moved to Ithaca to teach at Cornell. Loughran O'Connor created the cover for the Tender Buttons edition of *Trimmings*. She is a painter who had moved to New Jersey from California around the same time that I moved to the state of New York. Kathy Morris, a photographer in Ithaca, made the author portrait for the back of the book, which also featured blurbs from Bernadette Mayer, Charles Bernstein, and Gwendolyn Brooks.

While I was at Cornell, Gil Ott invited me to read at Painted Bride Arts Center in Philadelphia and then asked to see the manuscript of my work-in-progress. Gil designed the cover of S*PeRM**K*T and contributed photographs of his local supermarket. Food from that market found its way to my stomach in some memorable meals with Gil and Julia. A few years later Gil agreed to publish *Muse & Drudge*. By then I was at the University of Rochester with a Rockefeller Fellowship at the Susan B. Anthony Center. With help from artist Judy Natal, I designed the cover for *Muse & Drudge* using a photograph by Gil's friend Harvey Finkle. Sandra Cisneros and Henry Louis Gates, Jr. volunteered to write blurbs for the book. By the time *Muse & Drudge* was published, I was back in California, teaching at UCLA. I recently found an old letter from Gil Ott, recalling our tour of the Mutter Museum during one of my visits to Philadelphia, when he showed me a jar containing the liver once shared by conjoined twins Chang and Eng. Gil survived a kidney transplant and fathered a lovely daughter before his life ended in 2004. His gifts to the world include his poetry, his humor, and his generosity to other poets.

Trimmings and S*PeRM**K*T are serial prose poems that use playful, punning, fragmented language to explore sexuality, femininity, and domesticity. These companion pieces began as my response to Gertrude Stein's simple yet elusive poetic prose. For years I had difficulty with Stein. After several unsuccessful attempts to read her, I found an entry into her work through her story "Melanctha" in *Three*

Lives. I was startled by the liberties she took with the literary stereotype of the "tragic mulatto" in "Melanctha," a possible influence on writers of the 1920s Black Renaissance through their association with Stein's friend Carl Van Vechten. Richard Wright noted that Stein was a catalyst for his own writing.

With my hard-won appreciation for Stein's work, I was interested in her meditation on the interior lives of women and the material culture of domesticity, focusing on the inanimate objects that find their way into the home. Her idiosyncratic verbal "portraits" of hats, umbrellas, cups, and cushions illuminate, animate, and eroticize the domestic space to which women traditionally have been confined. My books *Trimmings* and *S*PeRM**K*T* correspond to the "Objects" and "Food" sections of Stein's *Tender Buttons*. I share her love of puns, her interest in the stuff of life, and her synthesis of innovative poetics with cultural critique. However, my own prose poems depart from her cryptic code to recycle and reconfigure language from a public sphere that includes mass media and political discourse as well as literature and folklore. Although I've been inspired by Stein, I'm also interested in the collision of contemporary poetry with the language of advertising and marketing, the clash of fine art aesthetics with mass consumption and globalization, and the interaction of literacy and identity. Originally I had planned a trilogy, with a third volume corresponding to the "Rooms" section of *Tender Buttons*. Some of my ideas concerning home and homelessness went into a collaborative project with visual artist Yong Soon Min for the *Womenhouse* web site.

When I wrote *Muse & Drudge*, I imagined a chorus of women singing verses that are sad and hilarious at the same time. Among the voices are Sappho, the lyric poet, and Sapphire, an iconic black woman who refuses to be silenced. Diane Rayor had translated surviving fragments of Sappho's ancient Greek poetry into an American idiom that sounded to my ear like a woman singing the blues. So *Muse & Drudge*, in a sense, is a crossroads where the blues intersects with the tradition of lyric poetry, as well as a text for collaborative reading and an occasion to unite audiences often divided by racial and cultural differences. Parts of this poem have been set to music by composers T. J. Anderson and Christine Baczewska. While many readers perceive *Muse & Drudge* as a more insistently "black" text than the other two, I have written all of these works from my perspective as a black woman, which I believe is no less representative of humanity than any other point of view.

I am thankful that Claudia Rankine, Jeff Shotts, Fiona McCrae, Anne Czarniecki, and Katie Dublinski of Graywolf Press have given me the opportunity to recycle books that had initially small audiences, combining *Trimmings*, *S*PeRM**K*T*, and *Muse & Drudge* to produce *Recyclopedia*.

HM

Trimmings

Don't ask me what to wear.
attributed to Sappho

Becoming, for a song. A belt becomes such a small waist. Snakes around her, wrapping. Add waist to any figure, subtract, divide. Accessories multiply a look. Just the thing, a handy belt suggests embrace. Sucks her in. She buckles. Smiles, tighter. Quick to spot a bulge below the belt.

Lips, clasped together. Old leather fastened with a little snap. Strapped, broke. Quick snatch, in a clutch, chased the lady with the alligator purse. Green thief, off relief, got into her pocketbook by hook or crook.

Tender white kid, off-white tan. Snug black leather, second skin. Fits like a love, an utter other uttered. Bag of tricks, slight hand preserved, a dainty. A solid color covers while rubber is protection. Tight is tender, softness cured. Alive and warm, some animal hides. Ghosts wear fingers, delicate wrists.

Starving to muffler moans, boa scarfs her up. Feathers tickle her nose. Kerchief, fichu. Gesundheit.

Her red and white, white and blue banner manner. Her red and white all over black and blue. Hannah's bandanna flagging her down in the kitchen with Dinah, with Jemima. Someone in the kitchen I know.

Brimming over eye shades cool complexion, delicate hue,
the lid on, keeps a cool head under high hat.

A little tight, something spiked, tries on a scandal. One of a pair vamps it up with a heel. If the shoe fits, another mule kicking, a fallen, arch angel loses sole support.

Two shapely legs stretch, then run. Sheer magic, a box divided. One saw a woman cut in half, waving incredible feet.

A light white disgraceful sugar looks pink, wears an air, pale compared to shadow standing by. To plump recliner, naked truth lies. Behind her shadow wears her color, arms full of flowers. A rosy charm is pink. And she is ink. The mistress wears no petticoat or leaves. The other in shadow, a large, pink dress.

The color 'nude,' a flesh tone. Whose flesh unfolds barely, appealing tan. Shelf life of stacked goods. Body stalking software inventories summer stock. Thin-skinned Godiva with a wig on horseback, body cast in a sit calm.

Garters garnish daughters partner what mothers they gather they tether.

In folds of chaste petticoats, chupamirtos. In a red sack with a silk ribbon, hummingbird, whose tongue is sweet. Charm for love, a captive beat, a flutter. Hidden under ruffles, secret heart, a red pouch tied with silk.

A rich match fits a couple of gilded calves. Silk stockings glide up fine-tuned, high-toned thighs. Blue-vein stock requires noblessing, sitting pretty in lap de luxe.

Bare skin almost, underworn. Warm stitched-together soft torn toy. Stuffed and laced voluptuous imaginary mammal made of lovely lumps. Dear plump-cheeked plaything taken to bed and hugged in the dark.

Releases from valises. Scientific briefs. Chemists model molecular shadows structure mimic dancers. Shirt on the line, a flapper's shimmy shake in a silk chemise. A shift, a woman's movement, a loose garment of manmade fabric. Polly and Esther living modern with better chemistry.

Of a girl, in white, between the lines, in the spaces where nothing is written. Her starched petticoats, giving him the slip. Loose lips, a telltale spot, where she was kissed, and told. Who would believe her, lying still between the sheets. The pillow cases, the dirty laundry laundered. Pillow talk-show on a leather couch, slips in and out of dreams. Without permission, slips out the door. A name adores a Freudian slip.

Night moon star sun down gown. Night moan stir sin dawn gown.

Dress shields, armed guard at breastwork, a hard mail covering. Brazen privates, testing their mettle. Bolder soldiers make advances, breasting hills. Whose armor is brassier.

Mistress in undress, filmy peignoir. Feme sole in camisole. Bit part, petite cliché. Dégagé ladies lingering, careless of appurtenances. Longing pajamas, custom worn to disrobe. Froufrou negligee, rustling silk, or cattle. Negligent in ladies' lingerie, a dressy dressing down.

Girt, a good old girl got hipped. They thrive with wives, broad beams. Most worthy girth, providing firm. Foundations in midriff. Across (between) girdled loins, tender girders. Gartered, perhaps, struts. Stretching, a snap crotch.

Some panties are plenty. Some are scanty. Some or any. Some is ante.

Tiny binary aftermath figure. Navel baste playmates with ultimate breeder of nuclear families. Suburban bombshell shelters magazines of big guns aiming to sell inny things or nothing at all.

Step into gathered floral. Sashay and flounce out. At length, skirt's sweep, her furbelow. Or slit, tight. Gored, wrapped, young shirttail tucked. Cowgirl, hips suede. Leather fringe skirts, a border. A stiff, fine crinoline. Straight seams, hemmed, or binding. Warm hands, felt skirt. An issue of blood, she pleated.

Mum, dissembling girl, resembling cartoon mouse. Scant-ness forces a stand, she cannot bend.

Heartsleeve's dart bleeds whiter white, softened with wear. Among blowzy buxom bosomed, give us this—blowing, blissful, open. O most immaculate bleached blahs, bless any starched, loosening blossom.

Menswear, the britches. Rosie flies off the handle. Jeans so tight, she pants. Wants to cool out, slacks off.

Of what material softness folds to hold her, under when over, inside or out, where air is, makes a difference in motion, living here—or walking. Taking off, putting on her flimsy garment. Holes breathe, and swallow. Openings, hem, sleeve. Borders on edges where skin stops, or begins. Fancy trim. Sew buttons on, but they are slow to open flowers—imagine the color. Loose skirt, a petal, a pocket for your hand. My dress falls over my head. A shadow overtakes me.

When a dress is red, is there a happy ending. Is there murmur and satisfaction. Silence or a warning. It talks the talk, but who can walk the walk. Distress is red. It sells, shouts, an urge turned inside out. Sight for sore eyes, the better to see you. Out for a stroll, writing wolf-tickets.

Girl, pinked, beribboned. Alternate virgin at first blush. Starched petticoat besmirched. Stiff with blood. A little worse for wear.

The bride wore white. Posed in modest bodice a la mode. Cake with sugar rosebuds and white frosting. Everyone gets a piece. Off-color jokes, borrowed and blue. Her blush, tip of the iceberg, froze in layers of lace, in a photograph of her smile.

Cold feet, darned socks. Mismatched pair, the black sock and the blue sock. Male color blindness. A girl's thin ankles.

What's holding her up. Straps, laces. Garters, corsets, belts with laces. What's holding them up. If not straps, then laces. Buttons and bows, ribbons and laces set off their faces. Girls in white sat in with blues-saddened slashers. Laced up, frilled to the bone. Semi-automatic ruffle on a semi-formal gown.

Her feathers, her pages. She ripples in breezes. Rim and fringe are hers. Who fancies frills. Whose finery is a summer frock, light in the wind, riffling her pages, lifting her skirt, peeking at edges. The wind blows her words away. Who can hear her voice, so soft, every ruffle made smooth. Gathering her fluttered pages, her feathers, her wings.

Clip, screw, or pierce. Take your pick. Friend or doctor, needle or gun. A dab of alcohol pats that little hurt hole. Hardly a dimple is soon forgotten brief sting. Stud, precious metal. Pure, possessive ring. Antibody testifying with immunity to gold, rare thing. So malleable and lovable, wearing such wounds, such ornaments.

❧

Body on fire, spangles. Light to sequin stars burn out at both ends.

Cinderella highball cocktail frock. Plastered, shellacked, and laminated. Blind drunk hobbled home in a lame dress.

Bones knit. Skins pink, flush tight. White margin, ample fleshings. Out of character, full blush. Flushed out of hiding, pink in the flesh.

Gold chains, choker, ring her neck. Draw a bead, string it. Precious jewel, locket. Real pearl handles it, lacy-necked in the black. What rankles, she fakes it. Less than naked, strung out, stranded.

Akimbo bimbos, all a jangle. Tricked out trinkets, aloud galore. Gimcracks, a stack. Bang and a whimper. Two to tangle. It's a jungle.

Harmless amulets arm little limbs with poise and charm.

In feathers, in bananas, in her own skin, intelligent body attached to a gaze. Stripped down model, posing for a savage art, brought color to a primitive stage.

Chichi busy bodice with fancywork got filigreed and gold. Then plumed themselves in fancy dress and knit their brows to clothe the naked.

Punched in like slopwork. Mild frump and downward drab. Slipshod drudge with chance of dingy morning slog. Tattered shoulders, frayed eyes, a dowdy gray. Frowzy in a slatternly direction.

Duds, garbled garb. Misfits, women in breaches. Early bloomers or bluestockings, whose blue worsted wicked black dress, or a white none inhabits. Unholy Magdalene with her veil of tears.

Mohair, less nape to crown fluffed pillow. Fuzzyhead, down for a nap. Soft stuff of dreams in which she fluffs it.

Animal pelts, little minks, skins, tail. Fur flies. Pet smitten, smooth beaver strokes. Muff, soft, 'like rabbits.' Fine fox stole, furtive hiding. Down the road a pretty fur piece.

Opens up a little leg, some slender, high exposure. Splits a chic sheath, tight slit. Buy another peek experience, price is slashed. Where tart knife, scoring, minced a sluttish strut. Laughing splits the seams. Teeth in a gash, letting off steam.

Swan neck, white shoulders, lumps of fat. A woman's face above it all. Unriddled sphinx 'without secrets.' Alabaster bust, paled into significance. Clothes opening, revealing dress, as French comes into English. Suggestively, a cleavage in language.

Decorative scrap. A rib, on loan. Fine fabric, finished at edges. Fit for tying or trimming. Narrow band, satin, a velvet strip. A ribbon wound around her waist. A glancing bow. Red ribbon woven through her, blue-ribbon blonde. For valor, a shred of dignity. A dress torn to ribbons.

For frills, fancy crimps and shaves. Cuts curls, frail frounce. Smiles, curtsies, now only of women flexing a fondness. Plain as a broad steaming a wrinkle, takes out the starch. Frilled up to here, she starts sleeking. Flat, flatter, flatterer.

Gaudy gawks at baubles fondle tawdry laces up in garish gear, a form of being content.

Chaste, apprehended, collared and cuffed. Kept under wraps, as bridal veils visually haze precious, easily torn, gauzy romantic tissues. Thin threads lace into delicate, expensive fabrics woven and unwoven at night by patient spinsters with needles and scissors. Laced in, as fate would have it. Knots and the tiniest holes. Surgical cutting and sewing. Peeking as usual. Skin under lace. A thread, a net effect, a web to sleep in. A white nightgown, girl, child, baby, laced and unlaced. A ruffle, a frill. A pale piece of something, almost made of air.

Rapt babes in peekaboo webs. Preying widows, spiders in black weeds. Smoldering glance in a drop-dead dress. Witches burning at high stakes. Blackened virgins, selling the sizzle.

Hand in glove hankers, waves a white flag. Hand to mouth surrenders, flirts with hanky-panky.

Low impact, lateral moves. No new wrinkles favor grace to last past shoe chat. Old sneakers jog their memories. Cool heels, odd hours in the park. Whistling dogs and cars exhaust. Stopped in her tracks, that doffed hat knocks her socks off.

Shades, cool dark lasses. Ghost of a smile.

A fish caught, pretty fish wiggles for a while. A caught fish squirms. A freshly licked fish sighs. Gapes with holes for eyes. A wiggling fish flashes its display. A pattern over whiteness. Bareness comes with coverage for peeking through holes to see flesh out of water. Cold holes where eyes go. The sea is cold. Her body of foam, some frothy Venus. Or strayed mermaid, tail split, bleeds into the sea. With brand new feet walks unsteady on land, each step an ache.

What a little moonlight inside her pink silvery is softness condensing a glaze to repair a blister. Itches sit and silken, growing dearer to the wearer. Who would wear a necklace of tears. Inside her moonlight lining, tears were shed. Smooth tears, bitter water, a salted wound produced a pearl. A mother's luster manufactured a colored other. Pearl had a mother who cried.

Her ribbon, her slender is ribbon when to occupy her hands a purse is soft. Wondering where to hang the keys, the moon is manicured. Her paper parasol and open fan become her multiplication of a rib which is connected and might start a fire for cooking. Who desires crisp vegetables, she opens for the climate. A tomato isn't hard. It splits in heat, easy. It's seasonal. Once in a while there is heat, and several flowers are perennials. Roses shining with green-gold leaves and bright threads. Some threads do wilt after starching. She has done the starching and the bleaching. She has pink too and owns earrings. Would never be shamed by pearls. A subtle blush communicates much. White peeks out, an eyelet in a storm.

Thinking thought to be a body wearing language as clothing or language a body of thought which is a soul or body the clothing of a soul, she is veiled in silence. A veiled, unavailable body makes an available space.

S*PeRM**K*T

❧

This is no authority for the abuse of cheese.
Gertrude Stein

Lines assemble gutter and margin. Outside and in, they straighten a place. Organize a stand. Shelve space. Square footage. Align your list or listlessness. Pushing oddly evening aisle catches the tale of an eye. Displays the cherished share. Individually wrapped singles, frozen divorced compartments, six-pack widows all express themselves while women wait in family ways, all bulging baskets, squirming young. More on line incites the eyes. Bold names label familiar type faces. Her hand scanning throwaway lines.

With eternal welcome mats omniscient doors swing open offering temptation, redemption, thrilling confessions. The state of Grace is Monaco. A shrine in Memphis, colossal savings. A single serving after-work lives. In sanctuaries of the sublime subliminal mobius soundtrack backs spatial mnemonics, radiant stations of the crass. When you see it, you remember what you came for.

Pyramids are eroding monuments. Embalmed soup stocks the recyclable soul adrift in its newspaper boat of double coupons. Seconds decline in descent from number one, top of the heap. So this is generic life, feeding from a dented cant. Devoid of colored labels, the discounted irregulars.

Just add water. That homespun incantation activates potent powders, alchemical concentrates, jars and boxes of abracadabra. Bottled water works trickling down a rainy day watering can reconstitute the shrinking dollar. A greenback garnered from a tree. At two bucks, one tender legal portrait of Saint No-Nicks stands in for clean-shaven, defunct cherry chopper. Check out this week's seasonal electric reindeer luz de vela Virgin Mary markdowns. Choose from ten brands clearly miracle H-2-O. Pure genius in a bottle. Not municipal precipitate you pay to tap, but dear rain fresh capped at spring. Cleaner than North Pole snow, or Commander in Chief's hardboiled white collars. Purer than pale saint's flow of holy beard or drops distilled from sterile virgin tears.

Aren't you glad you use petroleum? Don't wait to be told you explode. You're not fully here until you're over there. Never let them see you eat. You might be taken for a zoo. Raise your hand if you're sure you're not.

Desperately pregnant nubile preferred stock girls deliver perfect healthy psychic space alien test tube babes, in ten or less, or yours is free, we guarantee.

It must be white, a picture of health, the spongy napkin made to blot blood. Dainty paper soaks up leaks that steaks splayed on trays are oozing. Lights replace the blush red flesh is losing. Cutlets leak. Tenderloins bleed pink light. Plastic wrap bandages marbled slabs in sanitary packaging made to be stained. A three-hanky picture of feminine hygiene.

Iron maidens make docile martyrs. Their bodies on the racks stretched taut. Honing hunger to perfect, aglow in nimbus flash. A few lean slicks, to cover a multitude, fix a feast for the eyes. They starve for all the things we crave.

Chill out a cold, cold world. Open frost-free fridget. Thaw and serve slightly deferred gratification, plucked from the frozone, hard packed as slab of ice aged mammoth. Cool cache stashed between carbon dated ziplocked leftovers and soothing multicolored safety tested plastic teething ring.

Kills bugs dead. Redundancy is syntactical overkill. A pin-prick of peace at the end of the tunnel of a nightmare night in a roach motel. Their noise infects the dream. In black kitchens they foul the food, walk on our bodies as we sleep over oceans of pirate flags. Skull and crossbones, they crunch like candy. When we die they will eat us, unless we kill them first. Invest in better mousetraps. Take no prisoners on board ship, to rock the boat, to violate our beds with pestilence. We dream the dream of extirpation. Wipe out a species, with God at our side. Annihilate the insects. Sterilize the filthy vermin.

A daughter turned against the grain refuses your gleanings, denies your milk, soggy absorbency she abhors. Chokes on your words when asked about love. Never would swallow the husks you're allowed. Not a spoonful gets down what you see of her now. Crisp image from disciplined form. Torn hostage ripening out of hand. Boxtop trophy of war, brings to the table a regimen from hell. At breakfast shuts out all nurturant murmurs. Holds against you the eating for two. Why brag of pain a body can't remember? You pretend once again she's not lost forever.

Nine out of ten docks trash paper or plastic. My shrink wraps securely stashed and shredded freshness re-enforced double baggage. All tidy toxic clean dregs folded down in dumps with safety improved twist-off tops. Crumpled sheets, sweating ammunition. A strychnine migraine is a p.r. problem. Every orifice leaks. No cap is tamper proof.

Chow down on all floors. Nuzzle shallow dishes. Swallow spittle lapping muzzles. Doggie style fashions better leather collars. Caressed pets milk bone bandits. Checkerboard square, clean as hound's tooth. Rub a rawhide bone up out back. See Rover choose a rubber toy over puppy kibble. Poodle grooming lather bothers a tick. A bomb goes off to rid a house of pests. Yet pets are loyal and true watch dogs take a licking while nestling birds feather bed and beak fast kisses. Cat nips flannel mouse. Kitty litters kittens.

Plushy soft tissues off screen generic rolls as the world turns on re-vivid revival rewinds reruns recycling itself. A box of blue movie equals smurf sex. Poor peewee couldn't shake it. Wished he had a bigger one. Per inch of clear resolution's color window, more thick squares snag a softer touch.

～

Two thousand flushes drain her white porcelana, chlorinsed with antistepton disinfunktant unknownabrasives, cleanliness gets next to.

In specks finds nothing amiss. Rubs a glove on lemony wood. But the gleam of a sigh at a spotless rinsed dish. Spots herself in its service, buffed and rebuffed. Shines on the gloss of bird's eye drop leaf maple tabletop. Pledges a new leaf shining her future polishing skills. The silver dropped at dinner announces the arrival of a woman at a fork. She beams at a waxing moon.

What's brewing when a guy pops the top off a bottle or can talk with another man after a real good sweat. It opens, pours a cold stream of the great outdoors. Hunting a wild six-pack reminds him of football and women and other blood spoors. Frequent channels keep high volume foamy liquids overflowing, not to be contained. Champs, heroes, hard workers all back-lit with ornate gold of cowboy sunset lift dashing white heads, those burly mugs.

Off the pig, ya dig? He squeals, grease the sucker. Hack that fatback, pour the pork. Pig out, rib the fellas. Ham it up, hype the tripe. Save your bacon, bring home some. Sweet dreams pigmeat. Pork belly futures, larded accounts, hog heaven. Little piggish to market. Tub of guts hog wilding. A pig of yourself, high on swine, cries all the way home. Streak o' lean gets away cleaner than Safeway chitlings. That's all, folks.

Well bread ain't refined of coarse dark textures never enriched a doughty peasant. The rich finely powdered with soft white flours. Then poor got pasty pale and pure blands ingrained inbred. Roll out dough we need so what bread fortifies their minimum daily sandwich. Here's a dry wry toast for a rough age when darker richer upper crust, flourishing, out priced the staff with moral fiber. Brown and serve, a slice of life whose side's your butter on.

A dream of eggplant or zucchini may produce fresh desires. Some fruits are vegetables. The way we bruise and wilt, all perishable.

Bad germs get zapped by secret agents in formulaic new improved scientific solutions. Ivory says pure nuff and snow-flakes be white enough to do the dirty work. Step and fetch laundry tumbles out shuffling into sorted colored stacks. That black grape of underwear fame denies paternity of claymate raisinets. Swinging burgers do a soft shoe, gringo derbies tipping Latina banana. Some giggling lump of dough, an infantile chef, smiles animatedly at his fresh little sis. They never gets a tan in the heartwarming easy bake oven because they is eternal raw ingredients for programmed microwavering half-baked expressions of family love.

Toe jam must 'cause jelly don't. Mink chocolate melts in you.

Champagne dreams wet shammy softy. Hands-on carwash, a pampering. Bathtub's a cheap vacation. Cruising her archipelago, laid back with turn-on pages. Emerged from placid stacked suds, hyperbolic exotic aisle of glamour bubbles. Pearl diver's paradise. All sparkling steel and spritzed crystal rubbed down clean to the squeak. A body with an interior rolls out sleek waxed shiny hard enameled. It takes her away, that seductive new smell, in fourteen flavors. She's cherry, just driving off the lot.

Eat junk, don't shoot. Fast food leaves hunger off the hook. Employees must wash hands. Bleach your needles, cook the works. Stick it to the frying pan, hyped again. Another teflon prez. Caught in the fire 'round midnight, quick and dirty biz. Smoked in the self-cleaning oven.

How anorexics treat themselves. Sucking slim mint for the breathless, rationed yet tingling indulgence. Over-counters prescribe themselves slighter than any other lifetime of fractioned unburned energy hands down all ads up. How fresh in your mouth to eat a sweet thought minus the need to work off guilt, to amortize the cost.

Slow ketchup, slower. Dark coffee, darker. Nice white rice. Meat is real. Clean meat. Trimmed, not bloody.

Past perfect food sticks in the craw. Curdles the pulse. Coops up otherwise free ranging birds whose plucked wings beat hearts over easy. Flapping aerobically, cocks walk on brittle zeros. They make and break and scramble to get ahead. Whisk the yokels into shape. Use their pecker order to separate the whites.

Seeds in packets brighter than soup cans, cheaper than lottery tickets, more hopeful than waxed rutabagas, promising order in alphabetized envelopes, dream startled gardens one spring day tore open. Sown in good dirt, fingered tenderly.

Ad infinitum, perpetual infants goo. Pastel puree of pure
pink bland blue-eyed babes all born a cute blond with no
chronic colic. Sterile eugenically cloned rows of clean rosy
dimples and pamper proof towhead cowlicks. Adorable
babyface jars. Sturdy innocent in the pink, out of the blue
packs disposing durable superabsorbent miracle fibers. As
solids break down, go to waste, a land fills up dead diapers
with funky half-life.

Refreshing spearmint gums up the words. Instant permkit combs through the wreckage. Bigger better spermkit grins down family of four. Scratch and sniff your lucky number. You may already be a wiener.

Hide the face. Chase dirt with an ugly stick. That sinking sensation, a sponge dive. Brush off scum on some well scrubbed mission. It's slick to admit, motherwit and grit ain't groceries.

Flies in buttermilk. What a fellowship. That's why white milk makes yellow butter. Homo means the same. A woman is different. Cream always rises over split milk. Muscle men drink it all in. Awesome teeth and wholesale bones. Our cows are well adjusted. The lost family album keeps saying cheese. Speed readers skim the white space of this galaxy.

Muse & Drudge

∽

Fatten your animal for sacrifice, poet,
but keep your muse slender.
Callimachus

Sapphire's lyre styles
plucked eyebrows
bow lips and legs
whose lives are lonely too

my last nerve's lucid music
sure chewed up the juicy fruit
you must don't like my peaches
there's some left on the tree

you've had my thrills
a reefer a tub of gin
don't mess with me I'm evil
I'm in your sin

clipped bird eclipsed moon
soon no memory of you
no drive or desire survives
you flutter invisible still

another funky Sunday
stone-souled picnic
your heart beats me
as I lie naked on the grass

a name determined by other names
prescribed mediation
unblushingly on display
to one man or all

traveling Jane
no time to settle down
bee in her bonnet
her ants underpants

bittersweet and inescapable
hip signals like later
some handsome man kind on the eyes
a kind man looks good to me

I dream a world
and then what
my soul is resting
but my feet are tired

half the night gone
I'm holding my own
some half forgotten tune
casual funk from a darker back room

handful of gimme
myself when I am real
how would you know
if you've never tasted

a ramble in brambles
the blacker more sweeter juicier
pores sweat into blackberry tangles
going back native natural country wild briers

country clothes hung on her all and sundry
bolt of blue have mercy ink perfume
that snapping turtle pussy
won't let go until thunder comes

call me pessimistic
but I fall for sour pickles
sweets for the heat
awrr reet peteet patootie

shadows crossed her face
distanced by the medium
riffing though it
too poor to pay attention

sepia bronze mahogany
say froggy jump salty
jelly in a vise
buttered up broke ice

sun goes on shining
while the debbil beats his wife
blues played left-handed
topsy-turvy inside out

under the weather
down by the sea
a broke johnny walker
mister meaner

bigger than a big man
cirrus as a heart attracts
more power than a loco motive
think your shit don't stink

edge against a wall
wearing your colors
soulfully worn out
stylishly distressed

battered like her face
embrazened with ravage
the oxidizing of these
agonizingly worked surfaces

that other scene offstage
where by and for her he descends
a path through tangled sounds
he wants to make a song

blue gum pine barrens
loose booty muddy bosom
my all day contemplation
my midnight dream

something must need fixing
raise your window high
the carpenter's here
with hammer and nail

what you do to me
got to tell it
sing it shout out
all about it

ketchup with reality
built for meat wheels
the diva road kills
comfort shaking on the bones

trouble in mind
naps in the back
if you can't stand
sit in your soul kitsch

pot said kettle's mama
must've burnt them turnip greens
kettle deadpanned not missing a beat
least mine ain't no skillet blonde

sue for slender
soften her often
mamiwata weaves
rolexical glitter

get a new mouth
don't care what it costs
smell that hot sauce
shake it down south

the purify brothers
clamor for rhythm
ain't none of they business
'til the ring is on the finger

breaks wet thigh high stepper
bodacious butt shakes
rebellious riddem
older than black pepper

déjà voodoo queens
rain flooded graves in New Orleans
sex model dysfunction
ruint a guest's vacation

figures with lit wicks
time to make a switch
rumba with chains removed
folkways of the turf

black dispatch do do run run
through graffiti brierpatch
scratch a goofered grapevine telegraph
drums the wires they hum

mad dog kiwi antifreezes
green spittle anguished folks
downwind skidrowed elbow greasers
monkey wrench nuts and bolts

my skin but not my kin
my race but not my taste
my state and not my fate
my country not my kunk

how a border orders disorder
how the children looked
whose mothers worked
in the maquiladora

where to sleep in stormy weather
Patel hotel with swell hot plate
women's shelter under a sweater
friends don't even recognize my face

tombstone disposition
is to graveyard mind
as buzzard luck
to beer pocketbook

the backwoods deflated whip
blank North American skies
rag dolls made of black scraps
with pearl button eyes

random diva nation of bedlam
headman hoodlum doodling
then I wouldn't be long gone
I'd be Dogon

down there shuffling coal
humble materials hold
vestiges of toil
the original cutting tool

splendid and well-made
presenting no disturbance
the natural order of things
between man and himself

try others but none lasted
a shame they went that way
missing referents murking it up
with clear actors lacking

too tough is tough enough
to walk these dirty streets with us
too loud too strong too black bad
too many desires you've never met

butch knife
cuts cut
opening open
flower flowers flowering

scratched out hieroglyphs
the songs of allusion
and even the motion
changing of our own violins

cough drops prick thick
orange ink remover inside
people eating tuna fish
treat the architecture to pesticides

elaborate trash
disparaged rags
if I had my rage
I'd tear the blueprint up

chained thus together
voice held me hostage
divided our separate ways
with a knife against my throat

black dreams you came
sleep chilled stuttering spirit
drunk on apple ripple
still in my dark unmarked grave

ain't cut drylongso
her songs so many-hued
hum some blues in technicolor
pick a violet guitar

emblems of motion
muted amused mulish
there's more to love
where that came from

heavy model chevy of yore
old time religion
low down get real down
get right with Godzilla

write on the vagina
of virgin lamb paper
mother times mirror
divided by daughter

soulless divaism
incog iconicism
a dead straight head
the spectrum wasted

dicty kickpleat
beats deadbeats
hussified dozens
womanish like you groan

belly to belly
iron pot and cauldron
close to home
the core was melting

head maid in made out
house of swank kickback
plaçage conquer bind
lemon melon mélange

if you've been in Virginia
where the green grass grows
did you send your insignia
up a greased flagpole

you used to hock your hambone
at a cock and bull pawnshop
got your start as a sideman
now you're big on your own

what makes tough muffins
pat Juba on the back
Miz Mary takes a mack truck in
trade for her slick black cadillac

la muerte dropped her token
in the subway slot machine
nobody told the green man
the fortune cookie lied

keep your powder dry
your knees together
your dress down
your drawers shut

a picture perfect
twisted her limbs
lovely as a tree
for art's sake

muse of the world picks
out stark melodies
her raspy fabric
tickling the ebonies

you can sing their songs
with words your way
put it over to the people
know what you doing

curly waves away blues navy
saved from salvation
army grits and gravy
tries no lie relaxation

some little bitter
spilled glitter
wiped the floor
with spoiled sugar

back dating double dutch
fresh out of bubble gum
half-step in the grave
on banana peels of love

devils dancing on a dime
cut a rug in ragtime
jitterbug squat diddly bow
stark strangled banjo

how you feel when it's windy
something blue on you
speak to the feeling
consolate your mind

many strong and soon
these seeds open wings
float down parachutes
then try one more again

copulation from scratch
kisses go down hard
no weekday self
makes it bleed

edges sharpened
remove the blur
enhance the image
of dynamic features

dark-eyed flower
knuckling under
lift a finger for her
give the lady a hand

not her hard life
cramped hot stages
only her approach
ahead of the beat

live in easy virtue
where days behaving send
her dance and her body
forward to a new air dress

a pad for writing
where dreams hit el cielo
crack the plaster fool mood rising
it's snowing on the radio

honey jars of hair
skin and nail conjuration
a racy make-up artist collects herself
in time for a major retrospection

her lady's severe beauty
and downright manner
enhance the harsh landscape
positioned with urban product

mule for hire or worse
beast of burden down when I lay
clean and repair the universe
lawdy lawdy hallelujah when I lay

tragic yellow mattress
belatedly beladied blues
shines staggerly avid diva
ruses of the lunatic muse

odds meeting on a bus
the wrecked cognition
calling baby sister
what sounds like abuse

you have the girl you paid for
now lie on her
rocky garden
I build her church

a world for itself
where music comes to itself
three thirds of heaven
sure to be raining

on her own jive
player and instrument
all the way live
the way a woman might use it

sugar shack full
of fat sweaty ladies
women of size with men
who love too much

what is inward
wanting to get out
prey to the lard
trying to pass for butter

cakewalk matrix
tapping the frets
dubbed and mastered
tucked into the folds

kiss my black bottom
good and plenty
where the doorknob split
the sun don't shine

it's rank it cranks you up
crash you're fracked you suck
shucks you're wack you be
all you cracked up to be

dead on arrival
overdosed on whatever
excess of hate and love
I sleep alone

if you were there
then please come in
tell me what's good
think up something

psychic sidekick
gimme a pigfoot
show me my lifeline
read me my rights

in Dahomey the royal umbrella
roof sky tree dome
heads up the procession of saints
balling the jack back home

framed in her snake-relief decorated doorway
bordered with zigzag deer legs
the notched beam is a stepladder
dried millet a sign of hospitality

this art is fast disappearing
indigenous pigments learned from their mothers
earth from the river
fingers and hands

men harnessed mules
rode hard put away wet
on the brine sea
unwed men toss and sweat

dark rain laden clouds
fragrant womb
from pyramid to palm
the black tide of mud

calabash of water
botanica Yoruba
latecomers to a potboiler
plot rebellion in the quarter

under the drinking gourd
they stood in a word
free despite thirst
lovely in their dust

torn veins stitched
together with pine needles
mended hands fix
the memory of a people

go ahead and sing the blues
then ask for forgiveness
you can't do everything
and still be saved

update old records
tune around the verses
fast time and swing out
head set in a groove

felt some good sounds
but didn't have the time
sing it in my voice
put words in like I want them

noise in the market
my mustang done slowed down
tore up bad now
put a ruination on it

bring money bring love
lucky floorwash seven
powers of Africa la mano
poderosa ayudame numeros sueños

restore lost nature
with hoodoo paraphernalia
get cured in Cuban by a charming
shaman in an urban turban

forgotten formula cures
endemic mnemonic plague
statisticians were sure
the figures were vague

sister mystery listens
helps souls in misery
get to the square root
of evil and render it moot

wine's wicked wine's divine
pickled drunk down to the rind
depression ham ain't got no bone
watermelons rampant emblazoned

island named Dawta
Gullah backwater
she swim she fish
here it be fresh

cassava yuca taro dasheen
spicy yam okra vinegary greens
guava salt cod catfish ackee
fatmeat's greasy that's too easy

not to be outdone she put
the big pot in the little pot
when you get food this good
you know the cook stuck her foot in it

they pass their good air
mixed with fresh fair
complex ions somewhere
frimpted frone she's stand alone

female of the specifically
human woman not called
by dog or dug by some tool — no fool who
takes stray pets or rakes implements for complements

what I do with my hats
they make their own parade
of float and glitter like birds
adorn the open umbrella

my dreams could take
advantage of me and no
one would tell me because
they don't know where to reach me

mothers have spawned
what warriors now own
cruel emblems and secrets
divulged only to the adept

signs in the heavens
graphemes leave the trees
turning over fresh pages
of notation: a choreography for bees

cooter got her back scratched
with spirit scribble
sent down under water
with some letters for the ancestors

the folks shuffle off
this mortal coffle and
bamboula back to
the motherland

why these blues come from us
threadbare material soils
the original colored
pregnant with heavenly spirit

stop running from the gift
slow down to catch up with it
knots mend the string quilt
of kente stripped when kin split

white covers of black material
dense fabric that obeys its own logic
shadows pieced together tears and all
unfurling sheets of bluish music

burning cloth in a public place
a crime against the state
raised the cost of free expression
smoke rose to offer a blessing

with all that rope they gave us
we pulled a mule out of the mud
dragging backwoods along
in our strong blackward progress

she just laughs
at weak-kneed scarecrow
as rainbow crow flies
over those ornery cornrows

everlasting arms
too short for boxers
leaning meaning
signifying say what

Ethiopian breakdown
underbelly tussle
lose the facts just keep the hustle
leave your fine-tooth comb at home

if your complexion is a mess
our elixir spells skin success
you'll have appeal bewitch be adored
hechizando con crema dermoblanqueadora

what we sell is enlightenment
nothing less than beauty itself
since when can be seen in the dark
what shines hidden in dirt

double dutch darky
take kisses back to Africa
they dipped you in a vat
at the wacky chocolate factory

color we've got in spades
melanin gives perpetual shade
though rhythm's no answer to cancer
pancakes pale and butter can get rancid

the essence lady
wears her irregular uniform
a pinstripe kente
syncopation suit

she dreads her hair
sprung from lock down
under steel teeth press gang
galleys upstart crow's nest

eyes lashed half open
look of lust bitten
lips licked the dusky
wicked tongued huzzy

am I your type
that latest lurid blurb
was all she wrote
her highbrow pencil broke

self-made woman gets
the hang—it's a stretch
she's overextended weaving
many spindly strands on her hair loom

walking through the alley
all night alone
stalked by a shadow
throw the black cat a bone

step off bottom woman
when the joint gets jinky
come blazing the moment
the hens get hincty

raw souls get ready
people rock steady
the brown gals in this town
know how to roll the woodpile down

dry bones in the valley
turn over with wonder
was it to die for our piece
of buy 'n' buy pie chart

hot water cornbread
fresh water trout
God's plenty the preacher shouts
while the congregation's eating out

women of honey harmonies offer
alfalfa wild flower buckwheat and clover
to feed Oshun who has sweet teeth
and is pleased to accept their gift

these mounts that heaven touched
saints sleep in their beds
distress is hushed by dream when
they allow the bird to lift their heads

ain't your fancy
handsome gal
feets too big
my hair don't twirl

from hunger call
on the telephone
asking my oven for
some warm jellyroll

if I can't have love
I'll take sunshine
if I'm too plain for champagne
I'll go float on red wine

what you can do
is what women do
I know you know
what I mean, don't you

arrives early for the date
to tell him she's late
he watches her bio clock balk on seepy time
petals out of rhythm docked for trick crimes

flunked the pregnancy test
mistimed space probe, she aborted
legally blind justice, she miscarried
scorched and salted earth, she's barren

when Aunt Haggie's chirren throws
an all originals ball
the souls ain't got a stray word
for the woman who's wayward

dead to the world
let earth receive her piece
let every dark room repair her heart
let nature and heaven give her release

moon, whoever knew you
had a high IQ until tonight
so high and mighty bright
poets salute you with haiku

fixing her lips to sing
hip strutters ditty bop
hand-me-down dance of ample
style stance and substance

black-eyed pearl
around the world girl
somebody's anybody's
yo-yo Fulani

occult iconic crow
solo mysterioso
flying way out
on the other side of far

the royal yellow sovereign
a fragile grass stained widow
black veins hammered gold
folded hands applaud above a budding

flat back green and easy
stacked for salt meat seasoning
some fat on that rack
might make her more tasty

a frayed one way slave's
sassy fast sashay
fastens her smashing essay
sad to say yes unless

your only tongue turns
me loose excuse my French
native speaker's opening act
a tight clench in the dark theater

software design for
legible bachelors
up to their eyeballs
in hype-writer fonts

didn't call
you ugly—said
you was ruined
that's all

pass the paperbag
whether vein tests
the wild blue
blood to the bone

spin the mix fast forward
mutant taint of blood
mongrel cyborg
mute and dubbed

poor stick doll
crucifix stiff
bent bird shutters
torn parasol

mellow elbow lengthy
fading cream and peaches
bleach burn lovingly
because she's worth it

ass is grassy ass is
ashy just like we do
such subtle cuts
clutter the difficult

trick rider circuitry
wash your mariney
lick and a promissory
end of story morning-glory

dressed as a priestess
she who carries water
mirrors mojo breasts
Yemoja's daughter

some loose orisha gathering
where blue meets blue
walk out to that horizon
tie her sash around you

how many heads of cowries
openmouthed oracles
drinking her bathwater
quench a craving for knowledge

kumbla of red feathers
tongues chant song
may she carry it well
and put it all down

tom-tom can't catch
a green cabin
ginger hebben
as ancestor dances in Ashanti

history written with whitening
darkened reels and jigs
perform a mix of wiggle
slouch fright and essence of enigma

a tanned Miss Ann startles
as the slaver screen's
queen of denial a bottle
brown as toast Egyptian

today's dread would awe
Topsy undead her missionary
exposition in what Liberia
could she find freedom to study her story

up from slobbery
hip hyperbole
the soles of black feet
beat down back streets

a Yankee porkchop
for your knife and fork
your fill of freedom
in Philmeyork

never trouble rupture
urban space fluctuates
gentrify the infrastructure
feel up vacant spades

no moors steady whores
studs warn no mares
blurred rubble slew of vowels
stutter war no more

get off your rusty dusty
give the booty a rest
you must be more than just musty
unless you're abundantly blessed

I can't dance don't chance it
if anyone asks I wasn't present
see I wear old wrinkles
so please don't press me

my head ain't fried
just fresh rough dried
ain't got to cook
nor iron it neither

you've seen the museum of famous hats
where hot comb was an artifact
now it's known that we use mum or numb our stresses
sometimes forget to fret about our tresses

heard about that gal
in Kansas City got meatballs
yes you shall have cake and eat
your poundcake on the wall

quickie brick houses
don't roll rickrack stones
or bats eyelashes rocks you
'til bric-a-brac's got no home

ain't had chick to chirp nor child to talk
not pot to piss in, no dram to drink
get my hands on money marbles and chalk
I'll squeeze 'til eagle grin, 'til pyramid wink

tussy-mussy mufti
hefty duty rufty-tufty
flub dub terra incog
mulched hearts agog

hooked on phonemes imbued with exuberance
our spokeswoman listened for lines
heard tokens of quotidian
corralled in ludic routines

slumming umbra alums
lost some of their parts
getting a start
in the department of far art

monkey's significant uncle
blond as a bat
took off beat path
through tensile jungle

dark work and hard
though any mule can
knock down the barn
what we do best requires finesse

frizzly head
gumbo clay
skull drudgery
mojo handyman

crow quill and India
put th' ink in think
black cat in the family tree
hairy man's Greek to me

krazy kongograms
recite the fatal bet
missiles of affection
dingbat flings brick velvet

bean pole
lightning rod
bottle tree
tall drink

go on sister sing your song
lady redbone señora rubia
took all day long
shampooing her nubia

she gets to the getting place
without or with him
must I holler when
you're giving me rhythm

members don't get weary
add some practice to your theory
she wants to know is it a men thing
or a him thing

wishing him luck
she gave him lemons to suck
told him please dear
improve your embouchure

tomboy girl with cowboy boots
takes coy bow in prom gown
your orange California suits
you riding into sundown

lifeguard at apartheid park
rough, dirty, a little bit hard
broken possum poke a possum
park your quark in a hard aardvark

a wave goodbye a girl
bred on the Queen Mary
big legged gal
how come you so contrary

let the birds pick her
make a nest of her hair
let the root man conjure
her to stare and stir air

sauce squandering sassy cook
took a gander bumped a pinch of goose
skinned squadroon cotillion filled
uptown ballroom with squalid quadrille

don't eat no crow, don't you know
ain't studying about taking low
if I do not care for chitterlings
'tain't nobody's pidgin

Hawkins was talking
while I kept on walking
now I'm standing in my tracks
stepping back on my abstract

if not a don't at least a before
skin of rubber chicken
these days I ignore
I'm less interested in

gaudy colors you flaunt
how loud you sirens behave
the man drowns in your salt
you revive him with a wave

restless born-agains
outlaw beat machines
yet the drums roll on
let the churchy femmes say amen

downhome quotes
the human figure
carries the vote
over dead signatures

tasty brown sugar molasses
accused of wide abandoned laughter
nothing left to lose or gain
delicate powder melts in the brain

ass can't catch
mere language
sings scat logic
talking shit up blues creek

no miss thing
ain't exactly rude
just exercising
her right to bare attitude

rope rash lads
rubber whiplashed
breakneck beauty
can be had

money's mammy mentions
some chit chat
getting paid
to take it like that

singed native skin
binging island sun
shines on shingles
shunning unhinged singles

ghetto-bound pretos
call on dark petro
powers that be fighting
when there's no money to lighten

historic old haunts where
creole servants get the door
or sweep up dusty graveyards
with zombi esprit décor

tropical fantasy
punany as you want to be
coked bottled bodies
with fantacide faces

mutter patter simper blubber
murmur prattle smatter blather
mumble chatter whisper bubble
mumbo-jumbo palaver gibber blunder

colored hearing colored
sounds darker
back vowels lower
down there deeper

churn and dasher
mortar and pestle
bumped your head
on a piece of cornbread

I didn't went to go
swing slow zydeco
so those green chariots
light your eyes up

massa had a yeller
macaroon a fetter
in his claptrap
of couth that shrub rat

sole driver rode
work hard on demand
he's the man
just as long as he can

outside MOMA
on the sidewalk
Brancusi's blonde
sells ersatz Benin bronzes

Joe Moore never
worked for me—oh moaner
you shall be free
by degrees and pedigrees

handheld interview cuts to
steady voice over view
extra vagrants gobble up the scenery
this camera's gonna roll all over you

discarded barnacled bard
grinning with bad dentures
remembering coonskin adventures
in your hackneyed backyard

solar flares scrambled
bell bottoms sunnyside
signal didn't she ramble
those black holes backslide

drippy tresses bagged
in plastic do-rag
sensible heel in execu-drag
whose dress sucks excess

O rose so drowsy in
my flower bed your pink
pajamas zig-zag into
fluent dreams of living ink

carve out your niche
reconfigure the hybrid
back in kitchen
live alone, buy bread

your backbone slip
sliding silk hipped
to the discography
of archival sarcophagi

pregnant pause conceived
by doorknob insinuation
and onset animal
laminates no DNA

manx cat rations
pussy got your tongue
angoraphobic X-man
sex kitten operation

blow hair died
a natural death
laid aside glory fried
flashing a panacea

her realness
was wild at the time
leastwise they tell me
it was legendary

chez lounge lizard
hip-hop hazard
master beats and breaks
baby's back-up aches

a strict sect's
hystereotypist hypercorrects
the next vexed hex
erects its noppy text

where whirly Saturn
turns worldly girls
wear curly perms
affirm natty pattern

chenille feely zeroes
fuzzy nooky fumble
your nu-nile omieros
our frondy jungle

lucky lucre dream dujour
a lotto numbing ventured dues
paid off a doler
and another don't

rap attacks your tick
cold fusion's licks
could make you sick
nobody's dying in this music

womanish girl meets mannish boy
whose best buddy's a doggish puppy
he dictate so dicty, she sedate so seditty
the girl get biggity when the boy go uppity

I'm down to Saint James Infirmary
getting tested for HIV
the needle broke, the doctor choked
and told me I'd croak from TB

did I say nobody's dying
well I lied, like last night
I was lying with your mama who was crying
for all the babies born in Alabama

marry at a hotel, annul 'em
nary hep male rose sullen
let alley roam, yell melon
dull normal fellow hammers omelette

divine sunrises
Osiris's irises
his splendid mistress
is his sis Isis

creole cocoa loca
crayon gumbo boca
crayfish crayola
jumbo mocha-cola

warp maid fresh
fetish coquettish
a voyeur leers
at X-rated reels

spaginzy spigades
splibby splabibs
choice voice noise
gets dress and breath

slave-made artifact
your salt-glazed poetry
mammy manufacture
jig-rig nitty-gritty

fast dance synched up so
coal burning tongues
united surviving ruin
last chance apocalypso

broke body stammering spirit
been worked so hard
if I heard a dream
I couldn't tell it

pipsqueak at sea
snail shell matrices
whirlwind gig
minkisi indigo

rose is off the bloomers
storm in the womb
an old broom scatters
shotgun rumor

hip chicks ad glib
flip the script
spinning distichs
tighter than Dick's hatband

buttermilk haystack
woodpile inkwell
darktown brierpatch
buckwheat bottom sugarhill

mulatos en el mole
me gusta mi posole
hijita del pueblo moreno
ya baila la conquista

chant frantic demands
in the language
bring generic offerings
to a virgin of origins

yes I've tried in vain
never no more to call your name
and in spite of all reminders
misremembered who I am

ghosts brush past
surprise arrival at
these states of flux
that flow and flabbergast

cross color ochre with stalk of okra
that prickly lover told her
she tastes like an Okie
yet lacks the rich aroma of a smoker

those cloudy days I'd fly
from the icy airport
while you tried to breathe life
into your bucktoothed scarecrow

if you turned down the media
so I could write a book
then you could look me up
in your voluminous recyclopedia

raped notes torn
as deep ones parted
the frank odor of the rodeo
the reason a person

pretend you don't understand
reckless letters I wrote
can't read my crooked hand
decode those cryptic notes

you were longing to belong
thoughts wander where have you gone
Zuli made her bed at home
that's why we don't get along

her red flag is flying
with bright sequins shining
her heart of swords
is its own reward

feed the spirits or they'll
chew on your soul
you'll be swallowed and digested
by a riled-up crocodile

married the bear's daughter
and ain't got a quarter
now you're playing the dozens
with your uncle's cousins

sitting here marooned
in limbo quilombo
ace coon ballooned up
without a parachute

use your noodle for
more than a hat rack
act like you got the sense
God gave a gopher

couldn't fold the tablecloth
can't count my biscuits
think you're able to solve
a figure, go ahead and risk it

when memory is unforgiving
mute eloquence
of taciturn ghosts
wreaks havoc on the living

intimidates intimates
polishing naked cactus
down below a bitter buffer
inferno never froze over

to deaden the shock
of enthusiastic knowledge
a soft body when struck
pale light or moderate

smooth as if by rubbing
thick downward curving
bare skin imitative
military coat made of this

mister arty martyr
a jackass to water
changing partners
in the middle of a scream

bereft of flavor
for lack of endeavor
he chooses a heifer
and loses forever

delirious boozer
he smoothes her sutures
removes a moocher
from her future

a thing of shreds and patches
hideous scarecrow she
puts teeth in any nightmare
of the man who sleeps with matches

slashing both your wrists
to look tough and glamorous
dead shot up in the art gallery
you can keep your shirt on already

while I slip into something more funkable
rub-a-dub with rusty man abrasions
was I hungry sleepy horny or sad
on that particular occasion

invisible incubus took up
with a cunning succubus
a couple of mucky-mucks
trying to make a buck

slandered and absurdly slurred
wife divorced her has-been
last man on earth hauls ass to the ash can
his penis flightier than his word

precious cargo up crooked alleys
mules and drugs
blood on the lilies
of the fields

drive by lightning
let Mississippi rip
catch some sense
if you get my drift

watch out for the wrecking crew
they'll knock you into the dirt
your attic will be in your basement
and you'll know how it feels to be hurt

a planet struck by fragments
of a shattered comet
tell it after the break
save it for the next segment

tabloid depravity
dirty snowball
held together
with weak gravity

"fool weed, tumble your
head off—that dern wind
can move you, but
it can't budge me"

he couldn't help himself
he couldn't help it
he couldn't stop himself
nobody stopped him

blessed are stunned cattle
spavined horses bent under their saddles
blessed is the goat as its throat is cut
and the trout when it's gutted

Jesus is my airplane
I shall feel no turbulence
though I fly in a squall
through the spleen of Satan

in a dream the book beckoned
opened for me to the page
where I read the words
that were to me a sign

houses of Heidelberg
outhouse cracked house
destroyed funhouse lost
and found house of dead dolls

two-headed dreamer
of second-sighted vision
through the veil
she heard her call

they say she alone smeared herself
wrote obscenities on her breast
snatched nappy patches from her scalp
threw her own self on a heap of refuse

knowing all I have is dearly bought
I'll take what I can get
pick from the ashes
brave the alarms

another video looping
the orange juice execution
her brains spilled milk
on the killing floor

if she entered freely
drank freely—did that not mean
she also freely gave herself to one and all—
then when was she no longer free?

we believed her
old story she told
the men nodded at her face
dismissing her case

debit to your race
no better for you — lost
gone off demented
throwing unevenhanded

disappeared undocumented workhorse
homeless underclass breeder
dissident pink collard criminal
terminal deviant indigent slut

riveted nailed to the table
crumpled muddied dream stapled
in her face mapped folded back
to the other side of the facts

that her body bleeds
is no surprise
a fragment bursts and color seeps
through her camouflage

bannered behind her
braid unfurled
extended she lean aiming
breaking the ribbon

kink konk crisp crinkle
my monkey's off his head
he wears my hat that
helps me think a little

zipped into high-tech overalls
suited to her lightfoot boots
kicking her heels up
and away beyonder

just as I am I come
knee bent and body bowed
this here's sorrow's home
my body's southern song

cram all you can
into jelly jam
preserve a feeling
keep it sweet

so beautiful it was
presumptuous to alter
the shape of my pleasure
in doing or making

proceed with abandon
finding yourself where you are
and who you're playing for
what stray companion

Harryette Mullen is the author of six previous books, including *Sleeping with the Dictionary*, which was a finalist for the National Book Award, the National Book Critics Circle Award, and the *Los Angeles Times* Book Prize. She is Professor of English and African American Studies at the University of California, Los Angeles.

Recyclopedia has been set in Electra, a typeface designed for Linotype in 1935 by William A. Dwiggins. Book design by Wendy Holdman, composition at Prism Publishing Center, and manufactured by Versa Press on acid-free paper.